Mostly Luck

Mostly Luck

Odes & Other Poems of Praise

Lorraine Healy

MoonPath Press

Copyright © 2018 Lorraine Healy

All rights reserved. No part of this publication may be reproduced, distributed, or transmitted in any form or by any means whatsoever without written permission from the publisher, except in the case of brief excerpts for critical reviews and articles. All inquiries should be addressed to MoonPath Press.

Poetry
ISBN 978-1-936657-41-4

Cover photo by Lorraine Healy

Author photo by Dianne MoonDancer

Design: Tonya Namura using Baskerville

MoonPath Press is dedicated to publishing the finest poets of the U.S. Pacific Northwest.

MoonPath Press
PO Box 445
Tillamook, OR 97141

MoonPathPress@gmail.com

For Gus & Mendieta
For Phoebe

I have been so very lucky...

Acknowledgements

My gratitude to the editors of the following publications, where some of the poems in this collection first appeared—sometimes in slightly different versions.

"Ode to July" was first published in the *Ghost Town Poetry* anthology, edited by Christopher Luna & Toni Partington, Fall 2010.

"Ode to the Full Moon Over Kennewick, Pasco, and Richland" was first published in the 2008 *Fishtrap Anthology*.

"Ode to Butterscotch Pudding" was published by *The Raven Chronicles*, Winter 2013.

"Ode To The Palouse At Harvest Time" was published online on Washington State's Poet laureate blog in 2013, selected by then WA Poet Laureate, Kathleen Flenniken.

"Ode to October" was first published in *WindFall*, Fall 2011.

"To the Elusive White Birches," "Ode to November," and "Wood Chopping" were first published on the online journal *Parchment & Quill*, November 2011.

"Ode to November" was nominated to *The Best of the Net* contest, sponsored by Sundress Publications.

"The Man Who Calls Me 'Doll'" was published by the *Briar Cliff Review*, vol. 24, 2012.

"Orpheus On Saratoga Passage in April," and "What She'd Say" were first published in *Soundings*, September 2009.

"Ode to Vicky's Goats" was published by *The Wide Shore* online journal, vol. 1, Spring 2014.

Enormous thanks to Fishtrap for the fellowship and to Hedgebrook for the residences— many of these poems were written, revised and organized under your auspices.

Contents

vii   Acknowledgements

  4   Oda a Pablo Neruda
  5   Ode to Pablo Neruda

I

11   Ode to July
13   Ode to the Full Moon Over Kennewick, Pasco & Richland, Washington
15   Ode to a Peach
17   Ode to August
19   Ode to The Palouse at Harvest Time
21   Ode to a Coyote Skull
23   Ode to September

II

27   Ode to September II
29   Ode to Butterscotch Pudding
31   Ode to Garlic
34   Ode to October
36   The Names of God
38   To the Elusive White Birches
39   Ode to November
41   Wood Chopping

III

45   The Man Who Calls Me "Doll"
47   Ode to December
50   To January
52   February's Child
55   To February
57   Ode to Vicky's Goats
59   What She'd Say

IV
63 Ode to Snow
66 To Mid-March
68 Ode to the Triggering Towns
70 To April
71 Orpheus Along Saratoga Passage in April
72 Hymn to the Cows
74 Ode to The Tulip *Buncheros*
76 April II
78 To May
79 Velvet
82 Noon at Holmes Harbor

Coda
85 To June
87 An Elegy

89 Notes & Gratitude

93 About the Author

Mostly Luck

Odes & Other Poems of Praise

I thought my life was mostly luck

Patrick Lane, "Letter to Red Lane"

Oda a Pablo Neruda

Padre Pablo que estás
en el polvo, en el cielo,
en el pasto de Chile,
en la ola indetenible del Pacífico,
tú que sabes de tener el alma
al sur, tú que mirabas
pájaros y eras instántaneo pájaro,
Pablo continental, cantera abierta,
hombre falible, falible, falible,
estabas hecho de madera de Concepción
y el cobre de tu sangre
le hablaba al cobre oculto de la mina.
Padre Pablo, madre Pablo,
huérfano bienamado, insatisfecho,
dónde no estás, dónde
no me espera tu sombra
en este luminoso invierno de Buenos Aires,
en la larga tarde verde
de mi isla en el norte,
adónde no llego y te encuentro primero,
ya en camino a otro canto,
paseando al perro fantasma
que te hizo desear la vida eterna
que no creías que existiera.
Padre Pablo, señor de lo elemental,
tus Odas mi cuaderno de bitácora:
he llegado a la edad de la alegría
y ya estabas tú con tus banderas de colores,
repartiendo la esperanza como pan
y enamorándote del sol y los faroles.
Roto de Chile, vecino, confesor:
todo lo que encontré en la playa
de tu océano venía de ti.
Decía así: el universo entero

Ode to Pablo Neruda

Father Pablo who art
in Chile's dust, in Chile's skies,
on Chile's grass,
over the unstoppable Pacific wave,
you who know
what it is like to have
a soul that faces South,
you who stared at birds
only to shapeshift into bird,
continental Pablo, open quarry,
fallible, fallible, fallible man.
You were made of Temuco timber
and the copper in your blood
spoke to the hidden copper in the mines.
Father Pablo, Mother Pablo,
well-loved orphan, unsatisfied,
where are you not, where
is your shadow not waiting for me
this luminous winter of Buenos Aires,
in the long green afternoon
of my island, in the North;
where do I not arrive
only to find you there,
already on your way to another song,
walking the ghost of that dog
who made you wish for an afterlife
you did not believe in.
Father Pablo, lord of the elemental,
your Odes my atlas:
I have arrived at the age of joy
and there you were with colorful flags,
giving hope away like loaves of bread,
falling in love with sun and street lamps.
You Chile's *roto*, my neighbor and confessor:

existe para ser cantado.
Hasta la culpa. Hasta la pena.
Tus deseos son órdenes,
o árboles, o prados.
Mientras nos quede algo por cantar,
los albañiles de la palabra
perderemos la noción del tiempo.
Que nos sorprenda siempre tu voz hecha lechuza
aquietándonos la luz,
diciendo noche, noche, noche.

everything I found on your ocean's beach
came straight from you.
It spoke like this: the whole universe
exists so it can be sung to.
Even sorrow. Even guilt.
Your wishes are commands,
or trees, or meadows.
While we have something left
to sing to, we word masons
will lose the sense of time.
Until your voice turns nightbird
to surprise us in the sibilant birches
chorusing dusk, dusk, dusk.

I

Ode to July

A yearling glides through the browning grass,
and bites of the nettles, bites, bites,
even as the woods keep calling him
back, and he makes an opening
in its wall of green, vanishes.

July says listen, listen.
In my hands the bulging emerald envelopes
of peas—when unsealed: five,
seven tiny planets.
Summer's message screams rejoice
even in this unstirring overcast morning,
July comes to burnish, July like God
says multiply and the tubers do,
rhizomes do, nasturtiums
do and do,
July which is worshipped with a colander
in hand, knees on the dry ground,
July says fill and fill and obeys itself

and where it dries the brittle sticks of raspberry
it whispers September, and where it purples
the air spilled with lavender its secret is safe,
July with a hand of rose and a hand
of Shasta daisy, and the last of the lambs born,
the nests denuded of robin chicks,
July rubbing itself on the rusty length of this buck,
princely in the deep brambles,
catchlights in his eyes already laden
with August
        the gold of a finch
on the gold of bent garlic
how hungry

the world is and July overflows
with its flashfloods of wheat,
July's handiwork keeps pounding,
its avalanche of fruit and weed,
July's merciless giving,
it goes sleepless, drunk on the scent of itself,
just like God,
July is God
                at its silliest,
July is God's tenderness
which suns itself next to the oblivious
grass snake, July insane for water
in the long dusks of its days
where some horses stand nostril to sidewind
under a puckered July moon.

Ode to the Full Moon Over Kennewick, Pasco & Richland, Washington
(an entirely too familiar, almost disrespectful address to the old girl herself)

up from the East, gigantic peach—
mamacita moon,
nailed to the sky, moon
of Sonora, Sinaloa, of Baja,
coming to perch now

over these Horse Heaven Hills,
over Yellepit and infant apples,
over ghostly carcasses
of busted '79 Chevrolets,
over la gente

eh, luna, where
are your papers,
luna panzona,
stuffed to such roundness,
sinvergüenza, temptress moon

luna de fiesta, luna
bejeweled, full of July,
a little tipsy,
what a moon, híjole,

look at you, luna comadre
with giant white purse
full of aspirins, full of nickels

you gorda del cielo
belly-dipping into two rivers,
perfect moon of a telenovela

come dawn, there rolls down
la luna borracha, cansada—
mind you don't get snagged
in the vineyards, in the orchard
trees—mind the brown-armed men

don't have to free you
tendril by tendril
from a quicksilver branch loaded
with nectarines

Ode to a Peach

it was you
on that tree—
the one Eve could not
resist
(let the world
keep blaming the blameless
apple
while you smile),
streaked with sun,
peach of glory,
sweetness and afternoon
collided
to make you,
buttocks of summer,
first fruit of my childhood.

In my grandfather's orchard,
your trees stood flocked
by the plums, some goldly see-through,
some red as beets,
by the apples that were too young
for the summer
and therefore uninteresting—
but you, fleshed white
or blushed and yellow,
you left a tell-tale trail
on our guilty chins,
always stealing the old man's
best fruit too early,
the ones he'd been eyeing
for jam jars, the ones
destined for pie.

This was in the time
before we met
the little monkey of the kiwi,
when all our universe of fruit
was peach and berry—
who wanted oranges
with their white entrails
and doubtful sweet?
who had heard
of a "bad" peach, ever?

There you go,
forever in your cotton dress,
armed to the leaf in fragrance,
colossal peach,
in your embarrassed beauty,
napping on a sunny windowsill
or waiting for simple syrup
to boil you down
to the memory of summer,
perfect no matter how,
you creek of sugar,
you cross of fire
and full moon.

Ode to August

The sun has browned us
into August. First fogs
bring the sadsack horns
of ships out on the Passage at dawn.
The neighbor's donkey beats
the old rooster to the morning.
There are some long, round sounds in August.

But how silently the stalk
becomes a dahlia, then a thousand,
their excessive heads claiming
the sight of everything.
And, quieter still, these old maids,
the gladioli, which I have come
to love, those flowers of funerals
where I grew up. Look at them,
pale mauve, so slightly ruffled,
shy aunts when the dancing starts
at a wedding, swaying together.

With every passing afternoon
light steals the green off of trees,
so the air is emerald and the ground
is leached. This year
August's blackberries remain
hard and obdurate, tight upon the vines,
onions come up from the soil
like outsized pearls.

One day of rain.
Two days of rain.
And then the sun returns,
something broken in its will. It stretches through

and through across the expanse
of August, but dawn
and dusk are already hiding in September.

On the ridge, an owl on a fence pole looks
this way then that, looks
North then South, just looks.
It makes its own wind as it opens
itself in flight, slow flapping
what's left of Summer.
It is useless to call August's name and wonder
where to seek. Look around, August
is lost to everything
but lavender, nasturtium, rose of Sharon.

Ode to The Palouse at Harvest Time
The Palouse, Eastern Washington State

In the beginning the sky
was blue and wheat was yellow,
the clumps of sage were their exhausted green,
and so the farmers said
let the barns be red, and the barns
were red.

Today the wheat is ready, a thread
beyond golden
except a summer storm rages in
its mess of purple clouds
and stops the day.

The old Danes and Swedes
are in the Farmers' Cemetery
where death suits their natural reserve.
Grey slabs for Petersens, Larsens,
for every blessed Hanson.
And here and there, a perfect garland
surrounds a lovely, tiny marble lamb—
splurge for a child of wheat-like hair,
stolen by diphtheria.

The afternoon leaches
the rust of rain out of everything,
until the dry stubble
bursts with cricket and grasshopper.
Again the world a spark away
from wildfire, one unconscionable
flick of lightning touching down,
one idiot match flung out
a car window and why

do we call them wild
these fires arsoned by thoughtlessness,
ours, God's?

Come sunset, an almost solid haze
rattles everything from here to the horizon:
the chemical ghost of weedkiller,
dust from ten thousand fallow fields,
over the silos, over the Quonset huts,
over everyone's sins.

Ode to a Coyote Skull

and what got to you,
trickster,
what stopped your handsome gait
in its tracks,
and how long did you lay
ridding yourself of yellow fur,
boiling yourself down
to this:
a triangular meeting of bone,
a few remaining teeth,
the bow of cheek
which encircles now only
an absence of eyes,

and weren't you quite
the fellow, weren't you
the lad—a cad, traipsing
through woods and orchards
in search of lunch,
of hen-house—if pushed
to shove, adventurous cats.

Two years ago, one
of your wives whelped
by the tall grasses
ten yards from the house
and for a few days
I heard the minuscule yips
of your children,
saw all twelve of them—
twelve!—lined up like toy soldiers
staring down my bewildered dogs,
who vacillated between eating them
and offering their dry tits.

Nobody knew the woods
like you, coyote—all
the scents of hunger,
every nest of fawn, each path
between fir and dusk.
Nobody sang more poignant
to the lazy moon
than you and your clan—
you beyond dog, you gypsy,
you almost wolf,
devil-may-care,
you devourer of night.

Ode to September
Southeastern Washington

Persephone sits all alone
in a field
lost in a drowse of yellow air. Anyone

could talk her into
the ground, any place of shade, a breath
beyond the wine of this afternoon.

In the orchard, between the rows
of trees, a stew of pits,
fermented fruit, feathers

off colliding birds.
Thousands of peaches wounded red
and oozing, as if stabbed by knives.

If she were to walk through them, touch
each gnarled tree-trunk like she used to,
her sandals squishing pulp and fruit skin,

her legs would glisten from ankle to knee.
Beyond the windbreak of poplars,
her mother's in the kitchen,

the steam of scalded mason jars
blinds her as she puts up
tomatoes, cans quart after quart

of nectarines. Pickles cucumbers,
the scent like a wall of vinegar, turmeric,
mustard seed prickling her eyes.

Where has this day gone? This month.
Her hands ache and her knuckles
week by week get squarer, odd.

But not her girl. The girl is perfect,
a bolt of pale pink gingham,
a bowl of rubyfruit, gold dust.

Even if her silences are new, made of dark flint.
Even through her piles of books
on vampires. And monsters.

Vampires. Hell, a passing
fancy. Fourteen. Who didn't?
Before she calls the child back in for supper,

Demeter hurries out
to see about the corn.

II

Ode to September II
the island

The old gods of September
are at their forge,
hammering copper
and leaf. Before it's day,
above the rows of Fall
cabbage, the soft fog hovers a little
shakily, like an ancient priest's
blessing hand.

It is September when mermaids
come close to shore—
enticed by mushrooms or the scent
of woodsmoke, who's
to say. Defeated, rhubarb splays;
the ghosts of peas dry
on their scaffolding.

Let it be September
for the old dog catching her last fly
with a perfect flick of tongue,
then let her wait in the noon sun
for the world to drip away.
Let it be September clear across
her grave, as she goes back to soil
under a small shoot of lavender.

We want the bolt of gold
that is September unrolled,
we want the heartbreak
deep in its shine.

But this September has been rubbery
with drizzle and dead begonias,
and soaked straw over the garden beds
empty of potatoes.

This September owes all of us
four melancholic Sundays.
It owes us the grapes and whatever
is under the grapes
which now has to stay unripe.

The North wind brings in
a stretch of clouds like fish skeletons
on the sunset side of sky.

We're done with dry.
What comes is overcast
and soft with rain.

Ode to Butterscotch Pudding

First thing I learned to cook
—standing on a small stool—
I had mixed the packet's sweet gold dust
with cold, cold milk
and then, over the gas stove,
slowly burned it, not wanting to disturb
the pot's bottom with the stirring
wooden spoon.
Ruined.
Burnt milk is a hell of its own.
My mother's irritation tilted
toward fury, tilted back.
My mother's irritation
needed no stirring.

Did I learn?
I learned.
Pressing flat on lumps
dissolved them. Gold dust
turned a pale innocent brown
and milk got thick and heavier
under the metronome of spoon.

Wean the girl child
from fairy tales
and give her alchemy.

Will she play the piano?
No.
Will she knit and sew, like her mother?
Witness her fingers'
plodding grace.
Hunger for stories
leads her to reading instructions.

First this,
then this:
a treasure hunt.
And a way to learn
about fire, about what burns.

My mother put a circle of batter
in a vault—an hour later
out came cake.
The oven was its own mysterious universe.
I was not allowed
to light its dangerous bowels.

But on the stove, the perfect ring
of gasfire was red on the inside,
blue on the outside, one hiss
and the touch of one match.
Once the brew thickened,
once it got a skin,
it was ready. It was visible.

Nobody else in the house
liked butterscotch pudding.
Whatever time it took
from dust in a box
to dumb heap of brown
in the refrigerator,
something had happened
for which I had no words.
Magic? Self-reliance? A raft of something
and a wooden spoon for oar.

Wanting to make, and making.
Already up to the gills
with mad intention.

Ode to Garlic

when the entire garden limps into deep sleep,
we go looking for you, rotund
mustacho'ed gentleman,
dressed for the weather in grey,
pale red, papery suits one on top of the other,
as if prepared for the onslaught
of winter, after the weeks you spent
gently swaying in the barn,
that Indian Summer dance
slipping towards the dry nights of September.

This is another harvest: only the most
robust of you
will do, and in the soil's delightful mathematics
from the one, many,
from one solid pyramid of clove
a full head.

You willing peasant of our crops, easy
going, good-naturedly you go
into the cooling soil, ready to spend
the length of a full human pregnancy
growing and multiplying
under a blanket of straw to keep
snow and frost at bay, out
of sight and out of mind—

down come the winter rains, the spells
of icy Northern wind, who
remembers you? Not your aristocratic
cousins, shallot, scallion, leek,
not even the more democratic onion,
all waiting for the monochrome short days
to lengthen and to color;

not even I, looking out past the leached straw
still covering you, will give you
a second thought until unfailingly
you bring March in by its horns
taunting the wind with green
as you peek through, unrepentant,
ready for light

and for companions, like oh, your friends
the peas, unafraid of soil packed dense
with memories of below freezing,
and those other hard-working peasants,
the potatoes—all of you
asking for almost nothing, all of you
no trouble, willing to be;

without the tomatoes' and cucumbers'
alacrities, without the peppers'
needy cradle inside the house.

You push through weeds,
amiable garlic, you chug through the months
fattening in the dark while your hair
wilds and yellows as the Summer crests,
you will always yield without a trace of shyness,
ample of scent, pliable friend of the stove,
willing to go into anything, why not,
why not you say as you jump into the frying pan
to sing your torch song to the sizzling olive oil.

Foot soldier of Summer.
Never a prima donna, never diva.
Dependable, generous garlic,
I rue the childhood years I didn't welcome
your buttery abandon cloaked as pesto,

the way you candied by a slab of roast.
What did I know? You brought
the ancestral farmer out in me
and each year, each year, as July
collapses into August I grab you
by the long dry lengths, two handfulls,
two handbursts that I lift to cloudless skies

as if you were my success, I show you off
grateful that you kept your word,
the dirt you lived in still clinging to roots, unable
to let you go.

Ode to October
the island

Now that you are gone, October,
I can speak about the unlikely silks you shawled us with
this year, your random
truces. How I climbed the rope
of each day to the top
of the ridge, where my neighbor
burned the delicate remnants of summer
in his fire pit. How that made you
redolent of barn. And this:
you turned the does invisible,
you gave them the color of fir bark,
and an anemic slice of orange
called itself your moon.
The owls were full
of October words and night.
Along the ridge, each fern
became crimson and gold like the flags
of long-ago empires.
Oh, October, your fugitive promises.
Your threads—spider's gossamer, a rain
so thin and drizzly
it felt shredded.
Along both flanks of the island
the whales filed South, a sudden
spout of breath and sea
announcing them, the bobbing seals
collected and on guard
watching from just below
the water's skin.

Each morning mist in my mouth
and I in the mouth of
the mist, in the mouth
of the morning—October's mouth,
chilly but soft
with woodsmoke. October, you tease,
you heartbreaker. What
did you tell the birches,
what did you tell the alders?
Everything wanting to believe,
waterlogged raspberries, the leached-out
hollyhock, everything
allowed itself to be pruned.
Enough blue sky showed through
your lying pockets.
When you were done, your bells
kept tolling apples.

October, there are no
unnecessary days.

The Names of God

Once-a-month Margaret, in the middle
of the day, old eyes always afire, at my door
the blessed Margaret in her certainty
who tells me firmly God's one true name
is Jehovah—male God Jehovah, promiser
of a more perfect world.

Margaret, Margaret, I'm an impossible bone to gnaw.
I'll take your "Watchtowers" and read them,
the ones you draw from your
leatherette purse. That we could
go around with one name in our pockets
and trust it is God's. This broken world
so unrepentant while you,
mild Margaret, praise Jehovah's weather
and later in the car, carefully write up
details of our chat, so you won't forget to ask
next time, guile of the missionary.

Do you report about me at Kingdom Hall?
Am I your hard case on Goss Ridge Road?
Faith is such ore.
Its metal spine of truths can harden
so suddenly. My love of this place
is someone else's heresy. Your owning
the one true name of God impossible to me.
What if I call it leaf, or The Yellow,
the loving at the bottom of the well.
I am so afraid of righteousness,
what it does to our days.

Sweet Margaret, I believe that you believe
and what I believe stays
on this side of the open door
where I stand, well-mannered and appeasing,
polite. Perhaps
I should invite you in next time,
offer you hot tea, call you away
from this wooded hill
green with the greenness of a bewildering God.

To the Elusive White Birches

Between Tumwater Canyon
and a ghost town I look

for them. I want them
wet with drizzle,

soaked in fog,
their leaves already sun enough.

The paper peeling off
their icy bark.

I chase them,
ask them to be surrounded

by other trees' red
and gold.

I call out to them
and not one answer,

those birch bastards.

Their trunks of clouds
and chalk.

I ask them
to stay still

and they open their branches
to the uncharitable wind.

Ode to November

November, you brought me
into the world without fanfare,
you stole
my father who could not
have loved you more
and it was a different hemisphere
but it was you, November,
you who now shrugs off my grief,
my graying hair.

You made the jacarandás blossom
over Buenos Aires and anywhere I walked
their blue showered the broken
sidewalks and the city getting sorrier
by the year. Paths of tiny trumpets
almost violet with blueness, I didn't
want any other gift.

And here so far away you give me
everywhere-rain,
rain beyond clouds, rain falling sideways
and upwards—
and this year a load of wet snow
which you promptly froze over
and cold we could not chase away
with firewood
while my father's lonely bones in Buenos Aires
welcomed the tenth summer
over his grave.

No deal, November. I will never
trade my birth for his immense
death. He loved you dearly

and you took him out of a Sunday
dripping with sunlight,
made by the gods.

So you and I stay grey, November.
Unforgiven. Your thieving smile knocked
on a window pane that morning.
And stupid, stupid me, I swung it wide.

Wood Chopping

Before long,
the creek inside the wood
bursts, starts running—
and with each axe-down
the horses
trapped inside the wood
stampede wide
through the valley
of wood—all are sorrels—
and the oranges
tight inside the grain
come tumbling,
they fill the barn with swallows;
the rent wood and its camellias
which float on the skin
of the creek of wood
as it clefts
as it pounds—
before long,
the creek that was trapped
the horses that hid
in the yes tight
the wood's flaming oranges

III

The Man Who Calls Me "Doll"

In the high desert, he spends
the glazed nights on a maroon recliner
that understands his back
battered by the tractor.
Something new and filled with edges,
something lonely hides in the marrow
of his bones and soon will stream
his blood, and it will have its own call
which he doesn't want to heed.

Dowser man, the aluminum rod asleep
in the back of the truck now,
the soft shuffle of his steps over the ground
that hides a song of water and oil,
witching man who knew just where to dig
and how far, now left to dowse
the incomprehensible language of his turning blood,
mistrusting his own streams, old man finally
lamenting the seasons he will miss.

He is one of the concealed,
of the *tzadikim* who don't know
about themselves, how their goodness
steels the world for all of us,
how their humble, enduring gaze on everything
keeps us in foal, their hands calving
each wet day anew.

The last winter he'll have
settles over him. So many Advents
have come with their snow
chapping the palms of men like him,
out with the hay, out in the intemperate

darkness of day.
In silence he has mended
the small rips of God's forgetfulness:
the lame bum lamb, the frozen trough,
the bank taking the land.

What he can't say is how much,
how cussedly he has loved this world,
its tender creatures.

Ode to December

I

Here come the knives of December,
its broken mirrors, the air
filled with shards.
Then a rain which falls grey,
falls blue, falls grey.
Two sparrows perched on the wreck
of a hydrangea have been teasing
the pup since before light.
But then, everything
teases her: the wheelbarrow,
strings of water miraculously out
of the faucet, this pellet-like rain.
The North sky bands out
the color of fading bruises.

II

December's sly sun
with its bagfuls of empty
leaves the frosted grass untouched.
The pup's fur slowly fills
with the story of outside,
of dead water in ditches,
of dug soil around roots, and the chase,
and the chase.

And the chase.

III

There is a lone swallow perched
on a tuft of white-green
lichen on this
balmiest of Christmas days.

IV

December, you trudge over black ice
to where all sorrowful things
collect: the dismayed
addresses of the forgotten,
every book on origami,
broken baskets.
Greedy nights swallow
whatever's within reach,
prophets, oranges, the blameless.
So many Decembers when my hair
was brown, when I was
seafoam on a lover's chest.
A young dog sleeps at my side now,
brown as my youth. I count stars
'cause I can't name them.
I can't unlearn the Southern sky.
I think of dead friends who loved
summer. I wear reading glasses.
I lecture the sleeping pup
on García Lorca.

Outside, leaves on a bed
of dry hail look skeletal
and faded, as if plucked
from an ancient herbarium.

Air as thin
as steel wire. Hunger
starts calling every wild creature
by name.

To January

I

January will not let me sleep,
determined to break my whole heart
until I amble
under loaded skies, my breath thin,
my hands full of catastrophe.
Sayeth the Lord,
"Blessed be the joyless,
for they shall walk spent
and empty," and there is
some lightness in that.
All the sun does is touch
the tops of evergreens. Snow
dirties itself on the ground,
hardened, unlovely, unable
to disappear graciously.
Faultless snow.
But there we are.
Say you trade your love for hoarfrost;
you end up kissing every nostril
of the ice rain. Say you hide in a small hut
in the forest of your rage;
only ants will stumble on the path
that leads to finding you.
Sayeth the Lord "Punish your neighbor
as you would punish
your own sweet self."
I will take this hissy fit and call it
sorrow. I will shake my fist at January
and call for its bagpipers.

Write dirges, not an ode. Fuck odes.
January seems quite happy
ensconced in my leg bones.

II

We think we know grey
and then comes January.
Some days the ridge wears
fog like a jerkin
and voices from miles away
hang on the alders,
swaying with pale moss.

III

The young dog learns
that when snow melts
the earth gives back
the beef bones it had taken.

And now these plum-colored clouds
bursting with sleet
and with sleet the silence of white weather.
The moon's smallest finger
on the night's ice meadow.
The young dog wakes in the glow
of midnight, certain she's heard
the howl of day.

February's Child

1

This is no whirlwind.

It is a trudge through the ravine
of this night, then another.

On the bed, your mother is wrapped
by wide bands that somehow amplify
the wild gallop of your heart beat.
They are great gray swaths around her belly,
like the old sashes of St. Margaret's
the monks of St. Germain de Près
used to rent out to women ready to birth.

She has been pouring out a stream,
an ocean inside her which holds
you, lone tiny fish.
       She widens;
in the hinge of night, she is terror
and perineum, unappeased by ice chips,
only your father's hand tethers her
to the saner edges of this place
where she finds herself again, in disbelief.

2

You journey the tight inches, beyond
the peak of pelvic bone, splitting your mother
with your timid coming.

Little one, do you feel ambushed?
Did you ever suspect it would lead
into this, into cold,
into strident—in short, the world?

Outside, Horse Heaven Hills are bleached
by icy dew and full moon, February
has opened its door and in you come—
over 200 feather bones, a pink longitude,
lacking rage.

3

You of the short past: blastocyst
anchored in salt water, the swimming
tulip of the sperm, the languid egg
awaiting in the canyons of the fallopian tubes.

4

Still scaly, squirm of mauve, moon fish,
a crown of white membrane
clouding the whiskers on your head,
the cord which juts impossibly long,
unropelike, coiled as the line
of old fashioned dial telephones,

you look covered in wet talcum powder
but it is only the ruins
of your very first house,
stuck to your surprised skin,

that pearl grime that has also been your dress.
And there lies the deflated placenta
on a metal dish, ready for the fire
of hazardous waste. Your grandmother
won't plant it under a new tree, nor will you
get to say goodbye to the old friend.

5

Oh love, this is called air,
this invisible creek going inside you
and coming so neatly out.
This work.

Away from you, your splayed mother
is sewn back to her own fibers,
she and your Dad crane to where there are
no sounds of your wailing. To where you sleep,
spent of this first journey,
serene, swaddled, complete
in an acrylic see-through bassinette.

To February

The young dog throws her sable body
into the rhubarb's new red fingerlings,
each paw brimming with zeal,
with wonder.
Even in the stormiest grey there is
a lightness in February,
some element above the quilted clouds
refracting white
as if a monumental mill stone
had been pushed
a crack or two
and the room of the world
could be seen again,
down to its terrible corners.
A dark day in February
is an A-minor kind of day,
there is something
not lost, something can be
rescued—a plug of light
two or three yards beyond
the horizon but yes clearly there
or the coiled, contained force
of February's promises,
or its sheer bloody wind.
Who knows? It is a strange time,
February's perfect rectangular
shape, its clumps
of tight daffodils. Whatever
the engine of February is,
it is not absence
nor slow-waltzing sorrow
even in leap years, when February
adds a load of pine needles
to itself.

Though we walk this same road every day,
the dog, Zen monk of scent,
bows before every piece of scat,
last week's, yesterday's, last night's.
That which is pungent, is holy.

Nights have been clear
and flinty, the straw covering flowerbeds
stiff, brittle with frost.
But the soil underneath is a riot
of worms and desire, the horizontal speech
of rhizome spreading outward,
saying farther, saying soon.

Ode to Vicky's Goats

It is the time when they start dropping
in twos, in threes,
and some are a week old
and they bound on secret springs
and some a few minutes old,
sticky with afterbirth,
folded
tiny stunned packages under the ewe's legs.

There is no end to mud and cold
this February—Vicky
makes all the kids coats
from cut-off sweatshirts' sleeves
and they crowd out of the barn
to jump on cable-spool tables,
a spill of colored marbles
with minds of their own.

And I sit and become
another piece of furniture,
and they rain on me,
solid pellets of joy
in cotton envelopes,
who forgive the embarrassment
of my humanness and munch
on my bangs,
their nothing teeth and warm skinny tongues
suckling my fingers with right abandon.

The mothers headbutt my sides,
they too want human hands
scratching between their eyes,
their soft Nubian ears,

and my voice to praise their beautiful
children who now hang from their udders
like bell claps.

The world here smells of ammonia
and straw, of wet soil,
of goat upon goat. The immense
white sheepdog keeps his amber eye
on everything, head nested
on his outstretched paws.
I would like
to marry him.
I would like
that serene wet nose
on my shoulder when I wake.

And small goats in bright sweaters
butt him, bounce off him,
flip, climb as if the air
had holds in it,
all the air has is drizzle,
all the little goats need
is one corner of morning,
they can find a day's invisible ladders
on their own.

What She'd Say
for Maxine Kumin

In the wide overcast of this morning,
my dog snoring beside me,
I think of the old poet
unsentimental and hopeful with her bridal train
of dead beloved animals,

how she would take pleasure
in the blue Steller's jay out
of nowhere
who lights up the air,
the mad blue of him
two-stepping on the fence,
his head impossibly handsome,
opaque elegant black.
I wish everything in the world
were this blue, royal, indigo,
thatched upon, long feathered.

The one blue bird living on our acres,
searching for a bride, I think—
I like life paired solid—or, more
likely worms, Maxine would point out,
unafraid of beauty that needs to feed,
trusting the way we all compost ourselves.
She'd say doesn't the jay's head
look like an executioner's hood
as he flies back to his thin alder home.

IV

Ode to Snow

Hello, unannounced guest of late February,
of spent winter,
your four or five inches enough
to hush the world down
to its most basic whirr: birdsong
and cracks of overburdened alder limbs—
like patient, willing arms of ballerinas
who hold position until bonebreak.

In other places, I know, you
are serious, ruthless combatant.
But here you come armed with nothing
but a frilly nightgown, all tiptoe
and lace, shy maiden aunt
who'll only stay a day or two, if it's
no trouble.

And your morning light puts every
other light to shame, early dawn
lit like noon, sunup a lantern
on the firs, ferns caught in the act
of looking like hairy statues of themselves.

What a delay you bring, snow;
a few hours you let loose
upon the landscape and here we are
looking anew at the incline of our road,
thinking of neighbors, piling urgencies
to the side to walk with utmost
premeditation. Wheelbarrows of chopped wood,
cauldrons of soup, our needs have whittled.

The dog can barely put up
with the leash, your cloak has changed
the scents and moorings of her world.
What's this? And this? says every paw,
and more than ever today requires
she run with blind abandon
for the pure cold joy of it,
porch to barn and barn to porch
over and over—her almost-tail an engine:
let's walk all day.

The insistence of this air you brought,
sandpapering our faces—a reminder
that this late the woods are already
home to newborn, fawns, coyote pups;
that this cold makes everything hungrier—
even the marshes swallow up new ducklings—
that there is black ice
under your good intentions.

For two or three days
we needn't look at our sins. Overnight
you mercifully covered the clear-cut woods,
what we have poured over the fields.
The brown dog stops in mid-elation,
needing to chew off the diamonds
you've encrusted into her pads.

You bring an infantry of clouds down to our heights—
unglossy, impenetrable clouds now turned yellow,
now turned purple riveted to night skies.
This is you saying there is
more of you to come.

Months from now you will have seemed
impossible, a trick of the mind,
the small blue fire of you on our skins
a half-forgotten mirage as we squat
weeding Spring from awakened flower boxes;
in the green world we so yearned for,
overcome with want of white.

To Mid-March

The young dog's enthralled, nay,
enraptured by this whiff of Spring.
Pouncing on soil, she digs quick
furious holes,
paws on Earth's secrets.
Worms or voles, she knows something
is brewing within our hopeless
clay.
       The grass is green,
the moss is green,
it is St. Patrick's day.
One hundred nine years ago
my great-grandmother died birthing
a dead child, her tenth.
A time of hinge, mid-March.
Wind-wrought, filled
with wicked whim.

~~~

All day I have been looking at old photographs
and the dead have dutifully come.
My dead.
       I wish you could have known them.
And their dead,
the ones they'd loved and missed
and wished I'd met, as well.
And the lost landscapes
they had come from.

Their postcards, loops of cursive
and story. Why do they always
come mid-March? Is it
the pull of sap?

The camellias are late
and furled tight for a reason.
To the child filled with bee-swarm nightmares
every breeze turns into buzz.
What we fear becomes our syntax.

The last of my ancients
breathed her last
in sleep, last night. Here's a sentence:
her widest absence.

~~~

Is there a difference between pollen
and bone ash? This morning
I am gladly accepted by loss,
sorrow's terse hexagrams—

she died, he passed, she dropped dead,
someone's beloved dog is faring poorly.
The world and its irregular heartbeat.
And Spring comes verdant and wet, sputtering
like fire from unseasoned wood.

~~~

Young dog, full grown now,
she'll be this smallish, intent,
opinionated creature for many Marches,
wrecking the flower beds
with her prayerful nails.

Ode to the Triggering Towns

It is hard to be deranged by cities
and their chemical maladies
their neutral density
                  light

I only visit
                  anymore

and if I still get
the whole it   of it
their stacks of languages
and means of transportation
the clichéd
rush
                uncaring elbows
         film noir movie houses
the whole   quote unquote

oh satay kimchi enchilada
oh holy mackerel

let this be the ode
to the poem I can't write
                  not anymore

fragmentary
            broken
      faceted syntax
scratched emulsion

some things I still
>bus routes

>>the color of the sky the day
>>first jasmines go on sale
>>at the ever-green flower stalls

>>compass rose indivisible from bloodstream
>>this way North
>>>>turn
>>this way South

let this be the elegy
for the poem

I was given
with a wardrobe of aspirins
and matching scarves

It was left neatly tucked
behind a magazine kiosk
of a subway station
over which three railway lines

this can happen
any Thursday in late winter

the neck decides
all it wants around it
>>is the west wind

To April

And Spring found us
this last week of April,
alders and lilacs dotted
with almost not there leaf,
frail, translucent things
like the back of a newborn's knees.

And in hours the men unleashed
lawnmowers while we pondered
which potatoes to plant in the cold wet soil.
What comes is late and blanketed
in yellow pollen.

Some years it is like this,
April's recalcitrance
deters the tulips, blesses
slugs.

The pup leaps into bed
to announce the grey outside these windows
is indeed morning.
      Easter Sunday,
the wind's song is persistent.
It smells of soaked grass,
it speaks of resurrection.

Orpheus Along Saratoga Passage in April

Orpheus sings, bleeding ale
and woe for his love;
along this finger of sea,
the whales play his broken heart
back to him. The whales' song
is a song of those lost
to the underworlds. A song
of the sorrow at the depth
of no wave. What the music
spreads along the sand
looks like mist but feels
like gossamer. Which is to say,
the way this song works
is through enchantment.
The whale carries her song in
a pocket behind
the lovely boulder of her heart.
The song, along the shore,
looks like soft rain
but feels like the light of morning.
The way the whales work on Orpheus,
the way the music spreads
on the island, is through
conceit, a mirage of kindness.
Orpheus sleeps now,
he will ache forever.
The whales glide North
leaving their breaths behind.
It may look like mere air,
but their sighs falling on Orpheus
feel like a benediction: Eurydice's forgiveness,
like a trail of water
on its unstoppable way to cloud.

Hymn to the Cows
I love the cows best when they are a few feet away
    Gerald Stern, "Cow Worship"

Praise to these cows and the forgotten open gate
through which they heeded the voice
of early afternoon and sweet water creek,
praise their contented, round Hereford
selves on the hoof, up hill
away from everyone.
                        A night
around the trees, under April
rain, and not one
lowing.

Praise the old pail which I can fill
with cracked corn.
Praise the sensible remedy, for who
among us resists sweetness?

Their heads suddenly appear
in the small clearings between alder and fir,
floating like Chagall cows in the sky of Vitebsk,
but this is a green, green sky they float in
no less peacefully, they stare
deep in cow-thought.

Praise their demure eyes on the pail
in my hand, which I jangle, shins
in the mud and song in my call,
ah, vaca, vaca, vaca.... ay, vaca...
hey, cow...

And the happy avalanche of Big Red
butting my side while the muck holds me,
and the pail tantalizes
the pink and mauve rings of her nostrils,
as my hand offers a flat palm
of yellow.   Oh Red, why
would you have walked away
from this? The top of her head,
covered in dirty white curls, bobs
with such repentance. And Baby,
who resists bravely up the hill:
praise her stand for freedom and foraging.

Then Baby gets lured by Red's trot after the pail,
by what she can steal.
Now the violet tongues unfold
into their rightful troughs.
Praise their flesh
forever their own.

Praise the well-loved cows,
like twin dappled red cameos,
cows who will die of old age
with much grace, keeling
over into the kelly-green grass
on a day farthest from today—already
golden in cow memory, this day
prodigal cows found and feasted,
always welcomed and most
beloved when they were nearest.

Ode to The Tulip *Buncheros*

The boss has sent the whole crew
to these distant fields today;
one by one, they file out
off the decrepit school bus
and stand around their *capataz*
who explains what's what
in a braid of language mostly
Spanish, a few words of English,
and the new ones they have learned to birth.
"Gilberto, man, you are a *bunchero* today,"
the *capataz* says, and the rest look
at Gilberto who goes up one step
in the ladder of things.

The tulips nod to the breeze, so impossibly
full of themselves.

The crew goes up one to a row,
picking flowers that have bloomed
a breath over perfection. They have been taught
to be heartless. To detect
a line of wilt, a touch of slant.
They pluck. Gilberto moves between
rows, the blush hidden by his faded
cap, extending both arms towards
the squatting girls (he is
their two seconds of dream in a day
ankle-deep in Skagit Valley mud),
the bunch of less than perfect tulips
an evergrowing creature against his chest.
An easy haul gets them to the truck bed.
A *bunchero* today. By the time

the sun loses its chill, by eight,
he'll slap the cab roof once, twice,
and the brimming truck will go.

April II
No era la eternidad. Era la primavera
                Rosario Castellanos, "El resplandor del ser"

Days cleaved by a purple schooner made
of solid cloud
            and, on either side,
a tame blue afternoon.
The bees at work under delirious
deadlines, alder catkins
thick on the road—along which
my young dog sniffs out
the secret blueprint of Spring.

Where was all this light
before this week?
Hidden in gunny sacks, in the loft
of a barn, North of the North.
Whose gorgeous hand ripped burlap,
let it out?
I'm still too new to this place to know.

The air, you wouldn't call this
wind, moves fast
as it nips the ridge.
It is a week or two before the slugs.
Tulips and irises
have returned from exile.
Like the kind poor,
April gives of its little:
piecemeal growth. No extravagance.

A doorful of slowly warming light.
April's lean muscle,
its shy quiet heart.

~~~

But of course April is a liar—
within a day, it has let drizzle
back in. Returns contrite
with an armful of camellias
and the sun tied up with kite string.

~~~

When she caroms in late, the pup
smells of swamp and grasses,
of ditches running full.
Her scent of April night is blameless,
brimming with infinite frogs.

To May

May of lilac and forsythia,
May of the first true deep
cerulean sky,
May of the engines of grass
ceaselessly at churn.
May of cloud,
cloud, sun again. Warmth
like a sweet first kiss come
out of nowhere, then gone.
Summer playing its long game.

The nettles fortress up every random path
into the woods. Behind them,
a sometimes ditch and sometimes creek
unleashes pebbles which startle
the pup. The green here
has a sound of birds,
thrush, thrush, owl.
May on the trail at the end of our road:
horses have been through, have left
almost invisible signs, broken
alder branches, crushed ferns.
It is the young dog who has to tell you
they've been here, her almost tail
shaking,
her nose plowing the dirt.

Velvet
I was like turned turf in the breath of God,
Bog-bodied on the sixth day, brown and bare.
          Seamus Heaney, "The Tollund Man In Springtime"

From the bowels of the ridge,
her long bray of glee:
there's Velvet with bellows greeting the day
from inside of the threadbare shed
she shares with the pony.

Barely up the incline of September.
First fog just burned. The donkey's
expansive tongue tasting blackberries
in the air, sweetness carried in purple
to her delighted nostrils. I remember

the May noon I came outside,
to find her vertical face
in our petunias,
her smile of squared teeth
like old gigantic dice,
the soft cakes of her shit
on the driveway—

Velvet's sweet voice happy,
my own urging her back
home, thinking in vain of the halter
and bit we didn't have in the barn;
how hell no she wouldn't hear
of any human sense, how May
was astride on the back of mid Spring

and Velvet, who knew this, turned
driveway-down to the gravel
while I called my neighbor at work
to tell her the brown girl was out
and hoofing it down Goss Ridge
towards traffic and danger.

I followed her, a shadow
in the shape of a donkey
quick trotting into the dead-end of Goddell Road,
homesick for a path cutting some hill,
for the new green stalked by the ditches,
implausible pastoral Velvet, a spinster,
a dun, brown donkey perfect in her gait,

unstoppable that May noon swollen
with young thistles which must have been calling Velvet
away from whom she loves:
the two tow-headed children who kiss her muzzle
as soon as they jump
from the yellow school bus, riding her
up the driveway next to mine.

I never heard the end of the story.
I imagine the bog-bodied self of Velvet,
animated, drunk on the breeze
of adventure, roads of solitude,
Goss Lake pulling her thirst with Velvet
responding a trumpet-length of joy,
hee-haw, hee-haw, hee-haw

and the mouthfuls of nettles
and more steaming shit, her thanksgiving,
with no inkling of crownpiece or rein,
an animal broken with love, what is she thinking
as she trots up home again,
all gaskin and hock.

Noon at Holmes Harbor

Of course the great blue heron
doesn't know
the old dog is in no way a threat—

more grey than blue, taciturn eyes
fixed on the dog's golden abandon.
How can the antediluvian bird

guess this lope is the first arrow
away from grief, her first amble
out of the airless tent where we've been staying

since her brother dog was put to sleep?
The heron unfastens,
unfurls wings the span of windsails,

flaps once, flaps again.
Puts twenty yards of bay
between its perch

and dog. Who has stopped
to stare, her body
a yellow exclamation point.

The world
and all its herons,
its ambushes of joy.

Coda

To June

We came through the green hollows of June
        Kevin Barry, "City of Bohane"

I will absent myself.
I will absent myself.
I shall remove myself from thee,
June of stubble and cheap
corn whisky days.
Some years you can be
a spread bolt of cream linen
but they are few and far between.
I have had it with your empty
promises, your whiff
of summer, your bags
of rain. The slugs.
The weeds.

I shall remove myself from thee,
to the night by the cornfields
of Illinois to be deafened by cicadas.
I will go see the vast dust
of June across Oklahoma, Northern
Texas, the shadeless June
burning through New Mexico,
a blissful sun in pines
by Northern Arizona.

Or I will go farther, go love
the luminous June where I was born,
a proper winter June,
dry and transparent with a shard of cold.

But on the island you are
skittish like a dog in dream,

oh untrustworthy June—
look at you steal
the entire first week of July
for your own sorry
purposes.
        Be done.
Be gone while we keep
mowing your green hollows.

An Elegy

my neighbors today put up a cardboard sign
upon their fence announcing
Jenny, the girl donkey,
had succumbed to old age this sunny
fifteenth of June, and thanked us all
who had shared treats and attention
with the somewhat ornery (they
said goofy) Jenny, their beloved
these twenty-two years. Kind people
remember bits of carrot and apple given
to their creatures,
and even when they're grieving, will advise
those of us passing on foot
about the new absence in the pasture
where the four Shetland ponies, Jenny's
compadres, always more, shall we say,
personable than the late,
goofy Jenny, are still grazing
at a steady pace. Lately, Jenny had taken
to wearing a blue horse blanket
day in, day out, as the ponies' spectacular coats
mottled with rain. Perhaps that inner coldness
that comes with old age, perhaps a small
vanity in a light gray donkey
surrounded by horses out
of a fairy tale. History will tally
fourteen years of war out of the twenty-two
this donkey lived, plus uncountable
tragedies of every sort as well as the usual
human heartbreak. In the grand
scheme of things, a dead farm animal
amounts to not much. Not even

her good friends, the ponies, seemed to notice
on the pasture edged by Douglas firs
the shimmering hole in the air shaped like old Jenny.

Notes & Gratitude

"Ode to the Full Moon…" is for Luis Alberto Urrea.

"Ode to September I, Southeastern Washington" is for Eunice Oswalt Worden.

"Ode to October": the final line is in response to one in the poem "Evening in Tsarkoe Selo" in the book *This Lamentable City*, by Polina Barskova.

"Wood Chopping" owes much to Federico García Lorca.

"The Man Who Calls Me Doll" is for Bud Oswalt.

"February's Child" is for Kenzie.

"What She'd Say" is for Maxine Kumin.

"To Mid-March" contains a line by Lao Tzu.

A dozen years after leaving, I remain profoundly grateful to my beloved mentors at the New England College M.F.A. program: Paula McLain, Anne Marie Macari, Joan Larkin, and Alicia Ostriker, poets in residence Gerald Stern and the late Maxine Kumin, as well as the entire faculty in the years 2004-2006. A special thanks to Michael Waters and Mihaela Moscaliuc, also my teachers and friends at NEC, for their words on the back cover of this book.

After many years living the uncertain life of the legal immigrant, attorney Bonnie Stern Wasser's flash of inspiration and persistence allowed me to become the first poet ever to receive American residence (and now citizenship) through the merits of poetic work. My gratefulness to her knows no bounds, as well as to those big-hearted poets who wrote letters in support of my application: Gerald Stern, Alicia Ostriker, the late Tom Lux, Laure-Ann Boselaar, and Eleanor Wilner.

My family in Buenos Aires continues to support my writerly and photographic dreams with remarkable good humor and forbearance. My friends and first readers Diana Deering, Diane Divelbess, Janlori Goldman, and Sharon Shoemaker, made this a better book with their generous suggestions.

Almost twenty years ago, I received one of those hand-written, praiseful rejection letters that all writers dream of getting. The editor of a small press in New Hampshire told me to keep trying. Soon afterwards, upon being accepted to the NEC MFA Program, an out-of-the-blue phone call from that same editor, Lana Hechtman Ayers (who happened to be two terms away from graduation at NEC), gave me the best welcome anyone could hope for. Lana is the steadfast friend a poet needs, combining a sharp editing vision with a giving, openhearted understanding of the sustaining powers of poetry. I am proud to call her my editor and honored that we are friends.

Dianne MoonDancer proofread, edited, and whipped these poems into shape, plus walked the paths, cooked blackberries into every possible dish, and continues to stop the car anywhere to allow for many, many photographs to be taken. Her patience and kindness remain limitless.

Arriving late on a Halloween Night as a surprise gift, Miss Brown Dog sneaked her way into these odes in a matter of weeks. Slightly mellowed now, she remains enchanted by these woods. I am immensely grateful that she continues to drag me through them and deems me teachable in the art of paying attention.

About the Author

Lorraine Healy, award-winning poet and photographer, holds an M.F.A. from New England College and a post-M.F.A. in Teaching of Creative Writing from Antioch University, Los Angeles, as well as a Licenciatura in Modern Literature from her native Argentina. Called "one of the finest emerging poets" at work today by poet and critic Alicia Ostriker, Healy combines a solid grounding in the literary canon with an irrepressible playfulness with language and reverence for the natural world. In this second full-length book, Healy draws from the Spanish tradition of Machado, García Lorca, Hernández, Vallejo, and very especially, Neruda, to gaze upon her adopted Pacific Northwest landscape with luminous insight.

Healy was nominated for a Pushcart Prize in 2004 and was the first poet ever to receive American residence solely on the merits of her work. The winner of the 2009

Tebot Bach Prize, her first full-length volume *The Habit of Buenos Aires* was published in 2010, followed by the chapbook *Abraham's Voices* in 2014.

Lorraine's love for vintage and simple plastic film cameras has led to an extensive writing career in the world of analog photography. She lives on Whidbey Island, Washington, where she is at work on her next poetry book.

www.ingramcontent.com/pod-product-compliance
Lightning Source LLC
Chambersburg PA
CBHW020124130526
44591CB00032B/513